ALSO BY LES MURRAY

The Vernacular Republic: Selected Poems (1982)

The Daylight Moon and Other Poems (1988)

The Rabbiter's Bounty: Collected Poems (1991)

The Boys Who Stole the Funeral (1991)

Dog Fox Field (1992)

Translations from the Natural World (1992)

SUBHUMAN REDNECK POEMS

SUBHUMAN

REDNECK

POEMS

LES

MURRAY

Farrar, Straus and Giroux

NEW YORK

Farrar, Straus and Giroux
18 West 18th Street, New York 10011

Printed in the United States of America
Originally published in 1996 by Duffy & Snellgrove, Australia
Published in 1997 in the United States by Farrar, Straus and Giroux
First Farrar, Straus and Giroux paperback edition, 1998

Acknowledgments are due to the editors of the following
magazines and anthologies in which these poems first
appeared: The Adelaide Review, After Ovid—New
Metamorphoses, eds. Michael Hofmann and James Lasdun
(Farrar, Straus and Giroux), The Age, Akzente, Antipodes,
The Australian, The Bulletin, The Canberra Times, The
Colorado Review, Commonweal, Eureka Street, Five Bells,
Hobo, Image, The Independent Monthly, Lines Review,
London Underground posters series, Manuskripte, The
Mersey, Out West, ed. John Dale (HarperCollins
Publishers), Oxford Quarterly Review, Pequod, Planet,
P.N. Review, Poetry Kanto, Poetry Wales, The Printer's
Devil, Quadrant, Rialto, Salt, Scripsi, The Spectator, Spokes,
Studio, The Sydney Morning Herald, The Sydney Morning
Herald Good Weekend, The Sydney Review, Tablet, The
Times Literary Supplement, Ulitarra, Verse, and Voices.

The Library of Congress has cataloged the hardcover edition as follows:
Murray, Les A., 1938–
    Subhuman redneck poems / Les Murray.— 1st American ed.
    p. cm.
    ISBN-13: 978-0-374-27155-8 (hard : alk. paper)
    ISBN-10: 0-374-27155-0 (hard : alk. paper)
    I. Australia—Poetry.   I. Title.

PR9619.3.M83 S83   1997
821—dc21

                                        96049439

Paperback ISBN-13: 978-0-374-52538-5
Paperback ISBN-10: 0-374-52538-2

www.fsgbooks.com

P1

SUBHUMAN REDNECK POEMS

To the glory of God

for Salvatore Zofra

White grist that turned people black,
it was the white cane sugar
fixed humans as black or white. Sugar,
first luxury of the modernising poor.

It turned slavery black to repeat it.
Black to grow sugar, white to eat it
shuffled all the tropic world. Cane sugar
would only grow in sweat of the transported.

That was the old plantation,
blackbirding ship to commissar.
White teeth decried the tyranny of sugar—
but Italian Australians finished it.

On the red farm blocks they bought
and cleared, for cane-besieged stilt houses
between rain-smoky hills on the Queensland shore,
they made the black plantation obsolete.

When they come, we still et creamed spaghetti cold, for
    pudding,
and we didn't want their Black Hand on our girls.
But they ploughed, burnt, lumped cane: it shimmied like a
    gamecock's tail.
Then the wives come out, put up with flies, heat, crocodiles,
    Irish clergy,
and made shopkeepers learn their lingo. Stubborn Australian
    shopkeepers.
L'abito, signora, voletelo in sargia, do you?

Serge suits in Queensland? Course. You didn't let the white
    side down.
Shorts, pasta, real coffee. English only at school. But sweet
    biscuits,
cakes, icing—we learnt all that off the British and we loved it!
Big families, aunts, cousins. You slept like a salt tongue, in
    gauze.
Cool was under the mango tree. Walls of cane enclosed us and
    fell:
sudden slant-slashed vistas, burnt bitter caramel. Our pink
    roads
were partings in a world of haircut. I like to go back. It's
    changed now.
After thirty years, even Sicilians let their daughters work in
    town.

    Cane work was too heavy for children
    so these had their childhoods
    as not all did, on family farms,
    before full enslavement of machines.

    But of grown-up hundreds on worked estate
    still only one of each sex can be adult.
    Likewise in factory, and office, and concern:
    Any employee's a child, in the farmer's opinion.

We are the Australians. Our history is short.
This makes pastry chefs snotty and racehorses snort.
It makes pride a blood poppy and work an export
and bars our trained minds from original thought
as all that can be named gets renamed away.

A short history gets you imperial scorn,
maintained by hacks after the empire is gone
which shaped and exiled us, left men's bodies torn
with the lash, then with shrapnel, and taught many to be
lewd in kindness, formal in bastardry.

Some Australians would die before they said Mate,
though hand-rolled Mate is a high-class disguise—
but to have just one culture is well out of date:
it makes you Exotic, i.e. there to penetrate
or to ingest, depending on size.

Our one culture paints Dreamings, each a beautiful claim.
Far more numerous are the unspeakable Whites,
the only cause of all earthly plights,
immigrant natives without immigrant rights.
Unmixed with these are Ethnics, absolved of all blame.

All of people's Australia, its churches and lore
are gang-raped by satire self-righteous as war
and, from trawling fresh victims to set on the poor,
our mandarins now, in one more evasion
of love and themselves, declare us Asian.

Australians are like most who won't read this poem
or any, since literature turned on them
and bodiless jargons without reverie
scorn their loves as illusion and biology,
compared with bloody History, the opposite of home.

WHERE HUMANS CAN'T LEAVE
AND MUSTN'T COMPLAIN

for Becki and Clare

Where humans can't leave and mustn't complain
there some will emerge who enjoy giving pain.

Snide universal testing leads them to each one
who will shrivel reliably, whom the rest will then shun.

Some who might have been chosen, and natural police,
do routine hurt, the catcalling, the giving no peace,

but dull brilliance evolves the betrayals and names
that scar dignity and life like interior flames.

Hormones get enlisted, and consistency rehearsed
by self-avengers and failures getting in first,

but this is the eye of fashion. Its sniggering stare
breeds silenced accomplices. Courage proves rare.

This models revolution, this draws flies to stark pools.
This is the true curriculum of schools.

Poverty is still sacred. Christian
and political candles burn before it
for a little longer. But secretly

poverty revered is poverty outlived:
childhoods among bed-ticking midnights
blue as impetigo mixture, through the grilles,

cotton-rancid contentments of exhaustion
around Earth's first kerosene lamp
indoors out of wet root-crop fields.

Destitution's an antique. The huge-headed
are sad chaff blown by military bohemians.
Their thin metal bowls are filled or not

from the sky by deodorised descendants
of a tart-tongued womb-noticing noblesse
in the goffered hair-puddings of God's law

who pumped pioneer bouillons with a potstick,
or of dazzled human muesli poured from ships
under the milk of smoke and decades.

The mass rise into dignity and comfort
was the true modern epic, black and white
dwarfing red, on the way to green rose tan.

Green rose tan that the world is coming to,
land's colour as seen from space
and convergent human skin colour, it rises

out of that unwarlike epic, in the hours
before intellect refracts and disdains it,
of those darker and silver-skinned, for long ages

humbly, viciously poor, our ancestors,
still alive in India, in Africa, in ghettoes.
Ancestors, ours, on the kerb in meshed-glass towns.

That numinous healer who preached Saturnalia and paradox
has died a slave's death. We were manoeuvred into it by
      priests
and by the man himself. To complete his poem.

He was certainly dead. The pilum guaranteed it. His message,
unwritten except on his body, like anyone's, was wrapped
like a scroll and despatched to our liberated selves, the gods.

If he has now risen, as our infiltrators gibber,
he has outdone Orpheus, who went alive to the Shades.
Solitude may be stronger than embraces. Inventor of the
      mustard tree,

he mourned one death, perhaps all, before he reversed it.
He forgave the sick to health, disregarded the sex of the
      Furies
when expelling them from minds. And he never speculated.

If he is risen, all are children of a most high real God
or something even stranger called by that name
who knew to come and be punished for the world.

To have knowledge of right, after that, is to be in the wrong.
Death came through the sight of law. His people's oldest
      wisdom.
If death is now the birth-gate into things unsayable

in language of death's era, there will be wars about religion
as there never were about the death-ignoring Olympians.
Love, too, his new universal, so far ahead of you it has died

for you before you meet it, may seem colder than the favours
　　of gods
who are our poems, good and bad. But there never was a bad
　　baby.
Half of his worship will be grinding his face in the dirt

then lifting it to beg, in private. The low will rule, and curse
　　by him.
Divine bastard, soul-usurer, eros-frightener, he is out to
　　monopolise hatred.
Whole philosophies will be devised for their brief snubbings of
　　him.

But regained excels kept, he taught. Thus he has done the
　　impossible
to show us it is there. To ask it of us. It seems we are to be
　　the poem
and live the impossible. As each time we have, with mixed
　　cries.

Castle scaffolding tall in moat,
the dead trees in the dam
flower each morning with birds.

It can be just the three resident
cormorants with musket-hammer necks, plus
the clinician spoonbill, its long pout;

twilight's herons who were almost too lightfoot
to land; pearl galahs in pink-fronted
confederacy, each starring in its frame,

or it may be a misty candelabrum
of egrets lambent before Saint Sleep—
who gutter awake and balance stiffly off.

Odd mornings, it's been all bloodflag
and rifle green: a stopped-motion shrapnel
of kingparrots. Smithereens when they freaked.

Rarely, it's wed ducks, whose children
will float among the pillars. In daytime
magpies sidestep up wood to jag pinnacles

and the big blow-in cuckoo crying
Alarm, Alarm on the wing is not let light.
This hours after dynastic charts of high

profile ibis have rowed away to beat
the paddocks. Which, however green, are
always watercolour, and on brown paper.

Sex is a Nazi. The students all knew
this at your school. To it, everyone's subhuman
for parts of their lives. Some are all their lives.
You'll be one of those if these things worry you.

The beautiful Nazis, why are they so cruel?
Why, to castrate the aberrant, the original, the wounded
who might change our species and make obsolete
the true race. Which is those who never leave school.

For the truth, we are silent. For the flattering dream,
in massed farting reassurance, we spasm and scream,
but what is a Nazi but sex pitched for crowds?

It's the Calvin SS: you are what you've got
and you'll wrinkle and fawn and work after you're shot
though tears pour in secret from the hot indoor clouds.

Some of us primary producers, us farmers and authors,
are going round to watch them evict a banker.
It'll be sad. I hate it when the toddlers and wives
are out beside the fence, crying, and the big kids
wear that thousand-yard stare common in all refugees.
Seeing home desecrated as you lose it can do that to you.

There's the ute piled high with clothes and old debentures.
There's the faithful VDU, shot dead, still on its lead.
This fellow's dad and grandad were bankers before him, they
      sweated
through the old hard inspections, had years of brimming
      foreclosure,
but here it all ends. He'd lent three quarters and only
asked for a short extension. Six months. But you have to

line the drawer somewhere. You have to be kind to be cruel.
It's Sydney or the cash these times. Who buys the Legend of
      the Bank
anymore? The laconic teller, the salt-of-the-earth branch
      accountant,
it's all an Owned Boys story. Now they reckon he's grabbed a
      gun
and an old coin sieve and holed up in the vault, screaming
about his years of work, his identity. Queer talk from a bank-
      johnny!

We're catching flak, too, from a small mob of his mates,
inbred under-manager types, here to back him up.
      Troublemakers,

land-despoiling white trash. It'll do them no good. Their turn
is coming. They'll be rationalised themselves, made adapt
to a multinational society. There's no room in that for
    privileged
traditional ways of life. No land rights for bankers.

The paddocks shave black
with a foam of smoke that stays,
welling out of red-black wounds.

In the white of a drought
this happens. The hardcourt game.
Logs that fume are mostly cattle,

inverted, stubby. Tree stumps are kilns.
Walloped, wiped, hand-pumped,
even this day rolls over, slowly.

At dusk, a family drives sheep
out through the yellow
of the Aboriginal flag.

I work all day and hardly drink at all.
I can reach down and feel if I'm depressed.
I adore the Creator because I made myself
and a few times a week a wire jags in my chest.

The first time, I'd been coming apart all year,
weeping, incoherent; cigars had given me up;
any road round a cliff edge I'd whimper along in low gear
then: cardiac horror. Masking my pulse's calm lub-dub.

It was the victim-sickness. Adrenaline howling in my head,
the black dog was my brain. Come to drown me in my breath
was energy's black hole, depression, compere of the predawn
    show
when, returned from a pee, you stew and welter in your
    death.

The rogue space rock is on course to snuff your world,
sure. But go acute, and its oncoming fills your day.
The brave die but once? I could go a hundred times a week,
clinging to my pulse with the world's edge inches away.

Laugh, who never shrank around wizened genitals there
or killed themselves to stop dying. The blow that never falls
batters you stupid. Only gradually do
you notice a slight scorn in you for what appals.

A self inside self, cool as conscience, one to be erased
in your final night, or faxed, still knows beneath
all the mute grand opera and uncaused effect—
that death which can be imagined is not true death.

The crunch is illusion. There's still no outside world
but you start to see. You're like one enthralled by bad art—
yet for a real onset, what cover! You gibber to Casualty,
are checked, scorned, calmed. There's nothing wrong with
    your heart.

The terror of death is not afraid of death.
Fear, pure, is intransitive. A Hindenburg of vast rage
rots, though, above your life. See it, and you feel flogged
but like an addict you sniffle aboard, to your cage,

because you will cling to this beast as it gnaws you,
for the crystal in its kidneys, the elixir in its wings,
till your darlings are the police of an immense fatigue.
I came to the world unrehearsed but I've learned some things.

When you curl, stuffed, in the pot at rainbow's end
it is life roaring and racing and nothing you can do.
Were you really God you could have lived all the lives
that now decay into misery and cripple you.

A for adrenaline, the original A-bomb, fuel
and punishment of aspiration, the Enlightenment's air-burst.
Back when God made me, I had no script. It was better.
For all the death, we also die unrehearsed.

Time is told:
in the pot at the end of the rainbow

SUSPENDED VESSELS

for Joanna Gooding and Simon Curtis

Here is too narrow and brief:
equality and justice, to be real,
require the timeless. It argues
afterlife even to name them.

I've thought this more since that morning
in barren country vast as space-time
but affluent with cars
at the fence where my tightening budget
denied me basket-room
under the haunches of a hot-air balloon

and left thirteen people in it,
all ages, teens to grans,
laughing excitedly as the dragon nozzle
exhaled hoarse blazing lift, tautening it,
till they grabbed, dragged, swayed
up, up into their hiatus.

Others were already aloft,
I remember, light bulbs against the grizzled
mountain ridge and bare sky,
vertical yachts, with globe spinnakers.

More were being rigged, or offering
their gape for gusts of torch.
I must have looked away—
suddenly a cry erupted everywhere:
two, far up, lay overlapping,
corded and cheeked as the foresails of a ship
but tangled, and one collapsing.

I suppress in my mind
the long rag unravelling, the mixed
high voice of its spinning fall,
the dust-blast crash, the privacies
and hideous equality without justice
of those thirteen, which running helpers,
halting, must have seen
and professionals lifted out.

Instead, I look at coloured cash and plastic
and toddlerhood's vehement equities
that are never quite silenced.
Indeed, it prickles, and soon glares
if people do not voice them.

We had followed the catwalk upriver
by flowering trees and granite sheer
to the Basin park crying with peacocks.

After those, we struck human conversation.
A couple we'd thought Austrian proved to be
Cape Coloured. Wry good sense and lore

and love of their strange country
they presented us with, cheerfully.
They were eager "to get home for the riots."

As we talked, shoes dreamily, continually
passed above us on the horizontal chairlift.
It was Blundstones and joggers that year,

cogwheel treads with faces between them.
That was also the year I learned
the Basin was a cold crater lake:

swimmers whacking above ancient drownings—
"It's never been plumbed, in places."
I thought of a rock tube of water

down, down levels too frigid for upwelling,
standing at last on this miles-deep
lager head, above a live steam layer

in impossible balance, facing
where there can't be water, the planet's
convecting inner abortive iron star.

Higamus hogamus
Western intellectuals
never praise Auschwitz.
Most ungenerous. Most odd,
when they claim it's what finally
won them their centuries-
long war against God.

Four captured a man. When he grasped what they meant to
    do,
he stole the one's credit card and hid it in his shoe—
by which they were traced, after their butchery and howls,
and given a housewifely twenty years folding towels.

for Jonathan Hirschfeld

How Jews may have pioneered sculpture under Pharaoh's
    knout;
how atheism is sometimes a greater strictness about
the Second Commandment—ideas the massed green Tuileries
heard us stroll with, amid family lore, values by Worth, and
    fooleries,
pooped after your third session of translating my head into
    clay
preparatory to bronze. Not as Nature will do it someday.

Your intent travel through my features, transposing them to
    wet,
had half detached me from them. But I wouldn't start a new
    set
in that late headhunting capital. We came then to a netting-
    and-lath
builders' yard full of pedestals, giant jardinieres, torsoed
    wrath,
marble nymphs acid-eaten to plaster, bare matte heroes
standing whitely to reason, or weeping into their elbows.

It was so forlorn we couldn't help grinning. Poor cracked
discards of the ambient gloire, removed and stacked.
Did all universals, still expounding themselves with a
    clenched,
didactic or flat upsloped hand, get trucked there when
    retrenched,
to be one with lopped heads,. trophies of arms, carven
    terebinths?
There were no portraits in that corral of plinths.

No gargoyles either. Leaf-roofed, walled in high iron bars,
the grand dank gardens released us by a river of cars
streaming and cross-eddying, with sunk water in stanzas
    between.
Itching from the Shakespeare bookshop, I paused. Evolution
    seen
end on is creation. As often, every object seemed a case:
the great Louvre. Leash-dogs fighting. Six p.m. Back, impaled
in your studio, bulked our unbloodied milk-cocoa work face.

When Midas, no less deserving of mercy or better for
being a king dope, had lost all faith in the gods,
either they or their haughty absence sent him metaphor,

an ever-commencing order that can resemble a philosophy
but is more charming faster, like a bird that stars into flight,
like rhyme, its junior, like edgings of the clinker-built sea—

The gold was a symbol, like a need to prize things. I'm
    smarter
now! he cried. I'm enlightened, as befits a great king!
My silver age will not seize the taramasalata!

But his court worked like stuff he'd learned through
    nonhuman ears
and like a gold effigy entitled The Hug his first daughter
stood in the strongroom. Age was like age, tears like tears,

his palace equalled his design for it, and looked no nobler
    tiled,
his desire for slave girls was like when he could slake it,
his wife was like an aged queen, and his heir like a child.

Dried nests in the overhanging limbs
are where the flood hatched eggs of swirl.
Like is unscary milder love. More can be in it.

The flood boomed up nearly to the door
like a taxiing airliner. It flew past all day.
Now the creek is down to barley colour
waist deep on her, chest on him,
wearing glasses all around them, barely pushing.

Down under stops of deadwood pipe in living
branches, they move on again. The bottom
is the sunk sand cattle-road they know
but hidden down cool, and mincing
magically away at every step, still going.

The wide creek is a tree hall decorated
with drowned and tobacco ribbons,
with zippy tilting birds, with dried snakes hanging
over the doorways everywhere along.

They push on. *Say this log I'm walking
under the water's a mast like off a
olden day ship—* Fine hessian shade
is moistening down off cross-trees,

and like wings, the rocking waterline
gloving up and down their bodies
pumps support to their swimmy planet steps.

They've got a hook and bits
of bluebottle line from salt holidays.
They had a poor worm, and crickets automatic in a jar,
but they let all them off fishing.

They're taking like to an adventure instead,
up past there where the undercut bank
makes that bottling noise, and the kingfisher's
beak is like the weight he's thrown by
to fly him straight.

By here, they're wheeling stacked-up water.
It has mounted like mild ice bedclothes to
their chest and chin. They have to tiptoe
under all the white davits of the bush.

But coming to the island that is like the pupil
in acres of eye, their clothes pour water
off like heavy chain. They toil, and lighten
as they go up on it. All this is like the past
but none of it is sad. It has never ended.

WALLIS LAKE ESTUARY

for Valerie

A long street of all blue windows,
the estuary bridge is double-humped
like a bullock yoke. The north tide
teems through to four arriving rivers,
the south tide works the sinus channel
to the big heart-shaped real estate lake.
Both flood oyster farms like burnt floor joists
that islands sleep out among like dogs.

Glorious on a brass day the boiling up
from the south, of a storm above those paddocks
of shoal-creamed, wake-dolphined water.
Equally at dusk, when lamps and pelicans
are posted, the persistence of dark lands
out there on the anodised light void.

The northern shore used to be framed up
in shipbuilding's tap-tap and tar.
South across the wide celeste gap
where Lipariote fishermen Fazio and Sciacca

bagged nets, were a beacon, more shops, scallop
arches of a lattice pub, in another shire.
The Colonial Secretary, way back, gave not a rap
for that side's name, the Learning Place—blacks, hey?—

and wrote in his own name on the map,
but Pacific men, who'd built the North Coast railway,
became Koori there, warned off Town Beach by the cop.

On a punt like a fruit crate braced with wire
cars would balance for the crossing trip,
but the north side kept its name: Fish Shoaling in the Bay.

THE SAND DINGOES

Long before bridges, the old men who are hills now
were woken by the mopoke owl. And each had become an
    island,
ringed salt-white, like the bora. "Older sister, younger sister,"
they sang out, "you have drowned all our eastern country!"
"Yes, that Mopoke raped us! We turned him into a night bird
and dug up the salt water." The old men started whistling
and big sandy dingoes ran down from the blue plateau
far south, beyond the Wattagan. They streamed out past
    Barrenjoey
and swam all up the new coast. They yarded that wild ocean
to be lakes and swamps for the people's fishing, they lay down
around the old men on a cold night and still sleep there,
being new country in their pelts of tea-tree and palm,
there east of Left Hand, and Mixing Bowl, up east of
    Brisbane.
Those blue south mountains were halved in height, and the
    sisters
took their sea-digging sticks and camped with the Cross in the
    sky.

ON HOME BEACHES

Back, in my fifties, fatter than I was then,
I step on the sand, belch down slight horror to walk
a wincing pit edge, waiting for the pistol-shot
laughter. Long greening waves cash themselves, foam change
sliding into Ocean's pocket. She turns: ridicule looks down,
strappy, with faces averted, or is glare and families.
The great hawk of the beach is outstretched, point to point,
quivering and hunting. Cars are the surf at its back.
You peer, at this age, but it's still there, ridicule,
the pistol that kills women, that gets them killed, crippling
          men
on the towel-spattered sand. Equality is dressed, neatly,
with mouth still shut. Bared body is not equal ever.
Some are smiled to each other. Many surf, swim, play ball:
like that red boy, holding his wet T-shirt off his breasts.

LEASH CHAIN

The pelican of urban myth swooping
away with syllables of Chihuahua
leash-chain trickling from its beak
at the owner crying down the beach
can't have been more hunter-insouciant
than this wadded water-skier in bikers'
jacket wings now braking to assume
its seat on the lunchtime peak of tide.

Does that child's sock of dog, though, dropped
for its very chain, get pulled by it down
a boggling counter-chain to drowned zero?
Or does it rock back, tickling asphalt after
jerking fans across the floor of the palms'
idling forest of helicopter feathers?

FROM BENNETT'S HEAD

The absolute blue ocean is scaled and smoothed.
Fur seals, absolute until they die, ruche through it.

The headland mounts raked strata with a white-fronted
sea eagle angling along them. Inland, blue

medicinal scrublands are being bared and squared.
The wind brings a sense of shiplap and cream clinker.

It is the suburbs, broadcast in colour from Metropolis
and received along the coast by loans and savings,

the sort of money, not nobly notorious, which literary
language curls to ironise. But the sky is bare

of human class hatred. I mirror a blacktop street,
biscuit walls, Roman numeral balustrades, inner shadow

and a plastic pedal car, all fronting a vast minute clarity
of lives assuming brick, and not as a performance.

Take back Bohemia, Havel; take back the name.
Wrap it round the Hradčany, weight it with linden hills,
goose ponds and lozengy punchbowls. Let depression
find itself a new game.

Take back Bohemia, Vaclav. Don't supply a noun
to that dreamy world empire of unpaid and sexual police
where the tanks still are, green under boredom and garlands,
and fathers get mown down.

Take back Bohemia, dear President. Disclaim
the coffee machines whose every snort is *Bourgeois!*
where all non-Bohemians are cattle to brand, and all
difference is the same.

You alone, colleague, can close Bohemia back
down over Brno guns, plates of fox-with-juniper-berries
and that strategist of race whom Hindenburg's Bohemian
    corporal
sent upon you in black.

Reclaim Bohemia, Havel, and also Bohème
from that sweet soil, avid for barbed wire again,
where poetry is made a progressive model prison.
Now that Philistine is Palestine once more
take back your good name!

The impress of a whelk
in hard brown rock,

fluted as a plinth.
Its life gone utterly,

throb, wet and chalk,
left this shape-transmission,

a kin boat of fine brick.
Just off centre is a chip

healed before its death.
Before some credit help

this glazed biographee
beat surf-smash, stone rap,

maybe even saurid bite
in a swamp Antarctic.

Here, and where you are,
have been Antarctic.

It seems that merciless human rearrangement
of the whole earth is to have no green ending.
In khaki where nothing shoots back, rangers pose,
entering a helicopter with its sniping door removed.
In minutes, they are over drab where buffalo flee
ahead of dust—beasts rotund and beetle brown, with rayed

handlebar horns—or over shine that hobbles them in spray.
The rifle arrests one's gallop, and one more, and one,
cow, calf, bull, the two tons of projectile
power riding each bullet's invisible star
whipcrack their plunging fluids. Poor caked Asian cattle,
they lie, successive, like towns of salt stench on a map.

Passionate with altruism as ever inquisition was,
a statistical dream loads up for donkeys, cats, horses.
The slab-fed military rifles, with lenses tubed on top,
open and shut. A necked bulging cartridge case and animal
both spin to oblivion. Behind an ear, fur flicks,
and an unknowable headlong world is abolished.

But so far as treetops or humans now alive know
all these are indigenous beings. When didn't we have them?
Each was born on this continent. Burn-off pick and dusty
        shade
were in their memory, not chill fall, not spiced viridian.
Us against species for bare survival may justify
the infecting needle, the pig rifle up eroded gullies,

but this luxury massacre on landscapes draining of settlement
smells of gas theory. The last thing brumby horses hear

is that ideological sound, the baby boom.
It is the hidden music of a climaxing native self-hatred
where we edge unseeing around flyblown millions toward
a nonviolent dreamtime where no one living has been.

I was a translator in the Institute back
when being accredited as a poet
meant signing things against Vietnam.
For scorn of the bargain I wouldn't do it.

And the Institute was after me
to lose seven teeth and five stone in weight
and pass their medical. Three years I dodged
then offered the teeth under sacking threat.

From five to nine, in warm Lane Cove,
and five to nine again at night,
an irascible Carpatho-Ruthenian strove
with ethnic teeth. He claimed the bite

of a human determined their intelligence.
More gnash-power sent the brain more blood.
In Hungarian, Yiddish or Serbo-Croat
he lectured emotional fur-trimmers good,

clacking a jointed skull in his hand,
and sent them to work face-numbed and bright.
This was my wife's family dentist. He
looked into my mouth, blenched at the sight,

eclipsed me with his theory of occlusion,
and wrested and tugged. Pausing to blow
out cigarette smoke, he'd bite his only
accent-free mother tongue and return below

to raise my black fleet of sugar-barques
so anchored that they gave him tennis elbow.
Seven teeth I gave that our babies might eat
when students were chanting Make Love! Hey Ho!

But there was a line called Height-to-Weight
and a parallel line on Vietnam. When a tutor
in politics failed all who crossed that, and wasn't
dismissed, scholarship was back to holy writ.

Fourteen pounds were a stone, and of great yore so,
but the doctor I saw next had no schoolyard in him:
You're a natural weight-lifter! Come join my gym!
Sonnets of flesh could still model my torso.

Modernism's not modern: it's police and despair.
I wear it as fat, and it gnawed off my hair
as my typewriter clicked over gulfs and birch spaces
where the passive voice muffled enormity and faces.

But when the Institute started afresh
to circle my job, we decamped to Europe
and spent our last sixpence on a pig's head.
Any job is a comedown, where I was bred.

Blueing the blackened water
that I'm widening with my spade
as I lever up water tussocks
and chuck them ashore like sopping comets
is a sun-point, dazzling heatless
acetylene, under tadpoles that swarm
wobbling, like a species of flies
and buzzing bubbles that speed
upward like many winged species.

Unwettable green tacos are lotus leaves.
Waterlily leaves are notched plaques
of the water. Their tubers resemble
charred monstera trunks. Some I planted,
some I let float. And I bought
thumb-sized mosquito-eating fish
for a dollar in a plastic amnion.
"Wilderness" says we've lost belief
in human building: our dominance
now so complete that we hide from it.

Where, with my levered back,
I stand, too late in life,
in a populous amber, feet deep
in digesting chyle over clays,
I love green humanised water
in old brick pounds, water carried
unleaking for miles around contour,
or built out into, or overstepping
stonework in long frilled excess.

The hands' pride and abysmal
pay that such labour earned,
as against the necks and billions
paid for Nature. But the workers
and the need are gone, without reaching
here: this was never canal country.
It's cow-ceramic, softened at rain times,
where the kookaburra's laugh
is like angles of a scrubbing toothbrush
heard through the bones of the head.

Level water should turn out of sight,
on round a bend, behind an island,
in windings of possibility, not
be exhausted in one gesture, like an avenue.
It shouldn't be surveyable in one look.
That's a waterhole. Still, the trees
I planted along this one bend it
a bit, and half roof it, bringing
its wet underearth shadow to the surface
as shade. And the reeds I hate,

mint sheaves, human-high palisades
that would close in round the water,
I could fire floating petrol among them
again, and savage but not beat them,
or I could declare them beautiful.

Where will Australia be held?
Ethnics who praise their home ground
while on it are called jingo chauvinists.
All's permitted, though, when they migrate;
the least adaptable are the purest then,
the narrowest the most multicultural.

Where will we hold Australia,
we who have no other country?
Not Indigenous, merely born here,
shall we be Australian in Paraguay
again, or on a Dublin street corner?
Some of them like us in Dublin.

We were the proletarian evolution,
a lot of us. We've been the future
of many snobbish nations,
but now the elite Revolution
that rules unsullied by elections
has no use for us. Our experience
and presence, unlike theirs, are fictive
ideological constructions.

When we are made fully nothing
by our own, at home and abroad,
where will we hold Australia?
In con-men's scams? In overdone slang?
In great shifting floods and rescue?
In the hand-high spaces that doctors
crawled through beneath a wrecked train?

In the very uniqueness of a racism
practised only against ourselves?

For the moment, a salamander identity
is permitted us in fire, in the tones
that say, Well, we got all the kids out;
the house was only property;
where the unsleeping blood-eyed run

their hoses toward full nightmare,
saving strangers and strangers' houses
from the Other Flower of the gum tree,
feral highrise, blizzarding, total orange,
oncoming in shot azure, glorious as an air raid,
our recurrent Blitz, hideout of values.

He retains a slight "Martian" accent, from the years of single
  phrases,
He no longer hugs to disarm. It is gradually allowing him
  affection.
It does not allow proportion. Distress is absolute, shrieking,
  and runs him at frantic speed through crashing doors.
He likes cyborgs. Their taciturn power, with his intonation.
It still runs him around the house, alone in the dark, cooing
  and laughing.
He can read about soils, populations, and New Zealand. On
  neutral topics he's illiterate.
*Arnie Schwarzenegger is an actor. He isn't a cyborg really, is
  he, Dad?*
He lives on forty acres, with animals and trees, and used to
  draw it continually.
He knows the map of Earth's fertile soils, and can draw it
  freehand.
He can only lie in a panicked shout *SorrySorryIdidn'tdoit!*
  warding off conflict with others and himself.
When he ran away constantly it was to the greengrocers to
  worship stacked fruit.
His favourite country was the Ukraine: it is nearly all deep
  fertile soil.
Giggling, he climbed all over the dim Freudian psychiatrist
  who told us how autism resulted from "refrigerator"
  parents.
When asked to smile, he photographs a rictus-smile on his
  face.
It long forbade all naturalistic films. They were Adult movies.
If they (that is, he) *are bad the police will put them in
  hospital.*

He sometimes drew the farm amid Chinese or Balinese rice
terraces.

When a runaway, he made uproar in the police station,
playing at three times adult speed.

Only animated films were proper. *Who Framed Roger Rabbit*
then authorised the rest.

Phrases spoken to him he would take as teaching, and repeat.

When he worshipped fruit, he screamed as if poisoned when it
was fed to him.

A one-word first conversation: *Blane—Yes! Plane, that's right,
baby!—Blane.*

He has forgotten nothing, and remembers the precise quality
of experiences.

It requires rulings: *Is stealing very playing up, as bad as
murder?*

He counts at a glance, not looking. And he has never been
lost.

When he ate only nuts and dried fruit, words were for dire
emergencies.

He knows all the breeds of fowls, and the counties of Ireland.

He'd begun to talk, then returned to babble, then silence. It
withdrew speech for years.

Is that very autistic, to play video games in the day?

He is anger's mirror, and magnifies any near him, raging it
down.

It still won't allow him fresh fruit, or orange juice with bits
in it.

He swam in the midwinter dam at night. It had no rules about
cold.

He was terrified of thunder and finally cried as if in
explanation, *It—angry!*

He grilled an egg he'd broken into bread. Exchanges of soil-
knowledge are called landtalking.

He lives in objectivity. I was sure Bell's palsy would leave my
face only when he said it had begun to.

Don't say word! when he was eight forbade the word
"autistic" in his presence.

Bantering questions about girlfriends cause a terrified look and
blocked ears.

He sometimes centred the farm in a furrowed American
Midwest.

Eye contact, Mum! means he truly wants attention. It dislikes
I contact.

He is equitable and kind, and only ever a little jealous. It was
a relief when that little arrived.

He surfs, bowls, walks for miles. For many years he hasn't
trailed his left arm while running.

I gotta get smart! looking terrified into the years. *I gotta get
smart!*

I starred last night, I shone:
I was footwork and firework in one,

a rocket that wriggled up and shot
darkness with a parasol of brilliants
and a peewee descant on a flung bit;
I was busters of glitter-bombs expanding
to mantle and aurora from a crown,
I was fouettés, falls of blazing paint,
para-flares spot-welding cloudy heaven,
loose gold off fierce toeholds of white,
a finale red-tongued as a haka leap:
that too was a butt of all right!

As usual after any triumph, I was
of course inconsolable.

WAR SONG

translated from the German of Matthias Claudius, 1740–1815

It's war! O Angel of God, restrain
    It: lift up your voice!
It's war, alas—and unbearable pain
    If any think it my choice!

How would I endure it if, bloody and wan,
    The slaughtered came to me in sleep,
All those mourning spirits, and began
    Around me to weep?

If valiant men, maimed in the dust, near death,
    Who had gone seeking fame,
Writhed before me, and with their dying breath
    Cursed my very name?

If millions of poor fathers, mothers, wives,
    So glad before the war,
Now brought the wreck, the misery of their lives,
    Crying, to my door?

If famine, evil plague and their affliction
    Smote friend and foe the same,
Then stood up on a corpse to crow the fiction
    Of my glorious fame?

Neither in crown nor honour, lands nor gain
    Could I ever rejoice!
It's war, alas—and unbearable pain
    If any think it my choice!

AUSTRALIAN LOVE POEM

for Jennifer Strauss

A primary teacher taking courses,
he loved the little girls,
never hard enough to be sacked:
parents made him change schools.

When sure this was his life sentence,
he dropped studies for routine:
the job, the Turf papers, beer,
the then-new poker machine.

Always urbane, he boarded happily
among show-jump ribbons, nailed towels,
stockwhip attitudes he'd find reasons for
and a paddock view, with fowls.

Because the old days weren't connected
the boss wouldn't have the phone.
The wife loved cards, outings, "Danny Boy,"
sweet malice in a mourning tone.

Life had set his hosts aside, as a couple,
from verve or parenthood.
How they lived as a threesome enlivened them
and need not be understood.

Euchre hands that brushed away the decades
also fanned rumour
and mothers of daughters banned the teacher
in his raceday humour,

but snap brim feigning awe of fat-cattle brim
and the henna rinse between them
enlarged each of the three to the others, till
the boss fell on his farm.

Alone together then, beyond the talk,
he'd cook, and tint, and curl,
and sit voluble through rare family visits
to his aged little girl.

As she got lost in the years
where she would wander,
her boy would hold her in bed
and wash sheets to spread under.

But when her relations carried her,
murmuring, out to their van,
he fled that day, as one with no rights,
as an unthanked old man.

Inside Ayers Rock is lit
with paired fluorescent lights
on steel pillars supporting the ceiling
of haze-blue marquee cloth
high above the non-slip pavers.
Curving around the cafeteria
throughout vast inner space
is a Milky Way of plastic chairs
in foursomes around tables
all the way to the truck drivers' enclave.
Dusted coolabah trees grow to the ceiling,
TVs talk in gassy colours, and
round the walls are Outback shop fronts:
the Beehive Bookshop for brochures,
Casual Clobber, the bottled Country Kitchen
and the sheet-iron Dreamtime Experience
that is turned off at night.
A high bank of medal-ribbony
lolly jars presides over
island counters like opened crates,
one labelled White Mugs, and covered with them.
A two-dimensional policeman
discourages shoplifting of gifts
and near the entrance, where you pay
for fuel, there stands a tribal man
in rib-paint and pubic tassel.
It is all gentle and kind.
In beyond the children's playworld
there are fossils, like crumpled
old drawings of creatures in rock.

Mother and type of evolution,
the New Testament of the scholars
may be likened to a library catalogue
of the old type, a card index console
of wooden drawers, each a verse.
And you never know which ones are out,
stacked up, spilt, or currently back
in, with some words deleted
then restored. And it never ends.

Reputations slide them out,
convictions push them in.
Speculations look backwards once
and stiffen to salt-crystal proofs.
Dates grow on palms in the wilderness
and ferment in human minds—
and criticism's prison for all poems
was modelled on this traffic.

Most battered of all are the drawers
labelled Resurrection, The.
Bashed, switched, themselves resurrected
continually. Because it is impossible,
as the galaxies were, as life was,
as flight and language were. The impossible,
evolution's prey, shot with Time's arrow.
But this one is the bow of time.

Shadowy at a little distance tower
other banks of card-index drawers,

other myriad shelves, jammed with human names.
Some labelled in German are most actively
worked over, grieved, and reinserted.
More stretch away in Eastern scripts,
scarcely visited. Dust softens their head-words.
Yet the only moral reason to leave any
in silence fragments and reassembles
in the swarmed-over, nagged, fantasised
word-atoms of the critics' Testament.

The conquest of fire-culture
on that timber countryside
has broadcast innumerable
termite mounds all through
the gravel gold-rush hills
and the remnant railhead town,
petrified French mustards
out of jars long smashed.

Train platform and tin Shire
are beleaguered in nameless cemetery.
Outworks of the Dividing range
are annulled under Dreaming-turds.
It's as if every place a miner
cursed, or thought of sex,
had its abraded marker. Mile
on mile of freckled shade,
the ordinary is riddled by
cylinder-pins of unheard music.

On depopulated country
frail billions are alive
in layered earthen lace.
Their every flight is
a generation, glueing towers
which scatter and mass
on a blind smell-plan.
Cobras and meta-cobras
in the bush, immense black vines
await monsoon in a world
of clay lingam altars.

Like the monuments to every
mortal thing that a planet without God
would require, and inscriptionless
as rage would soon weather those,
the anthills erupt on verges,
on streets, round the glaring pub,
its mango tree and sleeping-fridges,
an estuary of undergrounds,
dried cities of the flying worm.

Surmounting my government's high evasions
stands a barbecue of crosses and birds
tended by a kangaroo and emu,
but in our courts, above the judge,
a lion and a unicorn still keep
their smaller offspring, plus a harp,
in an open prison looped with mottoes.

Coats of arms, plaster Rorschach blots,
crowned stone moths, they encrust Europe.
As God was dismissed from churches
they fluttered in and cling to the walls,
abstract comic-pages held by scrolled beasts,
or wear on the flagstones underfoot.
They pertain to an earlier Antichrist,

the one before police. Mafiose citadels
made them, states of one attended family
islanded in furrows. The oldest
are the simplest. A cross, some coins,
a stripe, a roof tree, a spur rowel,
bowstaves, a hollow-gutted lion,
and all in lucid target colours.

Under tinned heads with reveries tied on,
shields are quartered and cubed by marriage
till they are sacred campaign maps
or anatomy inside dissected mantling,
glyphs minutely clear through their one
rule, that colour must abut either
gold or silver, the non-weapon metals.

The New World doesn't blazon well—
the New World ran away from blazonry
or was sent away in chains by it—
but exceptions shine: the spread eagle
with the fireworks display on its belly
and in the thinks-balloon above its head.
And when as a half-autistic

kid in scrub paddocks vert and or
I grooved on the cloisons of pedigree
it was a vivid writing of system
that hypnotised me, beyond the obvious
euphemism of force. It was eight hundred
years of cubist art and Europe's dreamings:
the Cup, the Rose, the Ship, the Antlers.

High courage, bestial snobbery,
neither now merits ungrace from us.
They could no longer hang me,
throttling, for a rabbit sejant.
Like everyone, I would now be lord
or lady myself, and pardon me
or myself loose the coronet-necked hounds.

Now we face new people who share
attitudes only with each other,
withholding all fellowship with us,
and genial laughter. Reverse nobles
who twist us into Gorgon shapes
of an anti-heraldry, inside
their journals and never-lowered shields.

I came in from planting more trees.
I was sweating, and flopped down aslant
on the sofa. You and Clare were sitting
at the lunch table, singing as you do
in harmony even I hear as beautiful,
mezzo-soprano and soprano,
for anything Arno. You winked at me
and, liquescent as my face was,
I must have looked like the year
you painted all our portraits, lovingly,
exquisitely, on ceramic tiles
in undrying oil, just one
or at most two colours at a time,
and carried them braced oblique, wet,
in plastic ice-cream boxes to town.
It was encaustic painting,
ancient Rome's photography, that gets
developed in successive kiln firings
till it lives, time-freed, transposed
in behind a once-blank glaze.
Afterwards, you did some figured tiles
for our patchwork chimney, then stopped.
In art, you have serious gifts. But it's
crazy: you're not driven. Not obsessive.

At the edge of the tropics
they cut on the hills
raw shapes of other hills
and colour them banana.
One I used to see towering
each time I came away
climbed up and up, dressed in
a banana-tree beach shirt
with bush round its shoulders
like thrown-back jersey sleeves
and the rimmed sea below
drawing real estate to it.
Two islands were named Solitary
and the town wharf was crumbling
but surfers climbed sea-faces
on their boards, hand over hand.
The perched banana farms
mounted thousandfold stands
of room-long Chinese banners
or green to yellow lash-ups
of quill pens, splitting-edged,
their ink points in scrap vellum
each time I came away,
shiplapped fruit in blue mantles
all gaslit by the sun
and men drove tractors sidelong
like fighter planes, round steeps
worse than killed Grace Kelly.
Their scale came down to us
or caught round high-set houses.

I had shining hospitality
in dimmed subtropic rooms,
I unveiled a pastel school
and swift days keep passing
since I came away.

Most Culture has been an East German plastic bag
pulled over our heads, stifling and wet,
we see a hotly distorted world
through crackling folds and try not to gag.

Sex, media careers, the Australian republic
and recruited depression are in that bag
with scorn of God, with self-abasement studies
and funding's addictive smelling-rag.

Eighty million were murdered by police
in the selfsame terms and spirit which nag
and bully and set the atmosphere
inside the East German plastic bag.

It wants to become our country's flag
and rule by demo and kangaroo court
but it's wearing thin. It'll spill, and twist
and fly off still rustling Fascist! Fascist!

and catch on the same fence as Hitler, and sag.

Stopped by an earthquake on the North Coast line
in moonless dark, and thrumming, between Mount George
and Charity Creek, passengers become neighbours, worry,
peer out through mirrored selves. Opened doors reveal
steep winter canebrakes and the wide skinned scent
of the upper Manning River in a time of drought.
At the train's lit head, talk clangs like obscure tools.

Away over past a window is Kimbriki, tribal estate
of one dignified slim old man and the farm of another,
my great-great-grandfather. Both occupied the same land
amicably. Smoke rose beside separate bark roofings.
In the next generation, no tribal heir appeared.
What you presume concerning this will tell you
the trend of your life. The sky is bumper with stars:

each like a snowflake, if seen through reading glasses.
The crew still knocking out words up along the train,
the people beg for radios, telephones. It's an earthquake!
Miles out to the south my family already has news
but here we're baulked of action. All dark hills, no road.
Alarm is like childhood, when love was from before thinking.
Beyond choice, we see our loves as indigenes see land.

Kimbriki: pronounced KIM-brik-ai

Almost surprised to have been
delivered to the same house
as I went to sleep in, I unglue
my mouth and flap back the bedclothes.

Brickwork is dawning, and pooled streets
which are floors of that red sea.
Time enough, for descending stair-depths
on a smile, dispelling hosts' privacy.

The salmon were scabbard and blade
in the delis of Ireland;
mist formed like manna on dusk fields.
Glassed prison cells jutted singly

there, nuclei filled with soldiers
inside cubed membranes of mesh.
Wales was reached across tuned
high strings, and the proud black red cream

towns of England go orange at nightfall,
still being rammed by lorries,
all those cities that exiled and hanged
the present, when it was their future—

But the dream-tunnel I travelled in
to here was individual and is gone
forever into all I'll bring soon,
afresh, to that old collective, language.

Adult songs in English,
avoiding schmaltz,
pre-twang:
the last songs adults sang.

When roles and manners wore
their cuffs as shot as Or-
tega y Gasset's,
soloists sang

as if a jeweller raised
pinches of facets
for hearts as yet unfazed
by fatty assets.

Adult songs with English;
the brilliantine long-play
records of the day
sing of the singlish,

the arch from wry to rue,
of marques and just one Engel,
blue, that Dietrich played;
euphemism's last parade

with rhymes still on our side
unwilling to divide
the men from the poise,
of lackadays and lakatois—

and always you,
cool independent You,
unsnowable, au fait,
when Us were hotly two,

not lost in They.

Dousing the campfire with tea
you step on the pedal and mount
whip-high behind splashboard and socket.
Your burnished rims tilt and rebound
among bristling botany. Only
a day now to the Port,
to bodices in the coffee palace,
to metal-shying razors in suits
and bare ships towing out, to dress
and concentrate in the wind.

    Motoring down the main roads,
    fenced wheeltrack-choices in forest,
    odd scored beds of gravel,
    knotwood in the ground—
    you will have to wrestle
    hand and foot to reach Sydney
    and win every fall.
    River punts are respites.
    Croak-oak! the horsedung roads
    aren't scented any more, but tasted.
    Paved road starts at Chatswood:
    just one ferry then, to stringing
    tramcars and curl the mo,
    to palms in the wonderful hotels.

Blazing down a razorback
in slab dark, in a huge
American car of the chassis age
to rescue for pleated cushions

a staring loved one who'll sway
down every totter of the gangway
on cane legs. Petrol coupons
had to be scrounged for this one:
they have seen too much railway.

Queuing down bloody highways
all round Easter, crawling in
to the great herbed sandstone bowl
of tealeaf scrub and suburbs,
hills by Monier and Wunderlich
in kiln orange, with cracks of harbour,
coming down to miss the milking
on full board, with baked Sundays,
life now to be neat and dry eyed,
coming down to be gentrified.

One long glide down the freeway
through aromatic radar zones,
soaring Egyptian rock cuttings
bang into a newsprint-coloured
rainstorm, tweeting the car phone
about union shares and police futures.
Driving in in your thousands
to the Show, to be detained
half a lifetime, or to grow rental
under steel flagpoles lapping
with multicoloured recipes.

From just on puberty, I lived in funeral:
mother dead of miscarriage, father trying to be dead,
we'd boil sweat-brown cloth; cows repossessed the garden.
Lovemaking brought death, was the unuttered principle.

I met a tall adopted girl some kids thought aloof,
but she was intelligent. Her poise of white-blond hair
proved her no kin to the squat tanned couple who loved her.
Only now do I realise she was my first love.

But all my names were fat-names, at my new town school.
Between classes, kids did erocide: destruction of sexual
        morale.
Mass refusal of unasked love; that works. Boys cheered as
        seventeen-
year-old girls came on to me, then ran back whinnying
        ridicule.

The slender girl came up on holidays from the city
to my cousins' farm. She was friendly and sane.
Whispers giggled round us. A letter was written as from me
and she was there, in mid-term, instantly.

But I called people "the humans" not knowing it was rage.
I learned things sidelong, taking my rifle for walks,
recited every scene of *From Here to Eternity*, burned
        paddocks
and soldiered back each Monday to that dawning Teen age.

She I admired, and almost relaxed from placating,
was gnawed by knowing what she came from, not who.

Showing off was my one social skill, oddly never with her,
but I dissembled feelings, till mine were unknown to me too

and I couldn't add my want to her shortfall of wantedness.
I had forty more years, with one dear remission,
of a white paralysis: she's attracted it's not real nothing is
    enough
she's mistaken she'll die go now! she'll tell any minute she'll
    laugh—

Whether other hands reached out to Marion, or didn't,
at nineteen in her training ward she had a fatal accident
alone, at night, they said, with a lethal injection
and was spared from seeing what my school did to the world.

and Peter Wagner

Museums are an external brain
to hold what yours can't bear

and can't bear to let go.
Museums are terrible with There,

but mastered, on the walls. Not
still that age, amid the frozen urine,

thirst-wagons and soul-detaching fear.
Museums are numinous with Before:

the thumbed shawl waistcoats and organdie
that preceded the fall of the air.

Museums are also a fortress
in which you keep alive the Enemy

so that his descendants must come
to see what else made him jaunty.

but beware: preserve the defeated
and all the defeated win.

Only gone, beyond Pascal's wager,
is each person just as they are.

Don't die, Dad—
but they die.

This last year he was wandery:
took off a new chainsaw blade
and cobbled a spare from bits.
Perhaps if I lay down
my head'll come better again.
His left shoulder kept rising
higher in his cardigan.

He could see death in a face.
Family used to call him in
to look at sick ones and say.
At his own time, he was told.

The knob found in his head
was duck-egg size. Never hurt.
Two to six months, Cecil.

I'll be right, he boomed
to his poor sister on the phone.
I'll do that when I finish dyin.

—

Don't die, Cecil.
But they do.

Going for last drives
in the bush, odd massive

board-slotted stumps bony white
in whipstick second growth.
I could chop all day.

*I could always cash
a cheque, in Sydney or anywhere.
Any of the shops.*

Eating, still at the head
of the table, he now missed
food on his knife side.

*Sorry, Dad, but like
have you forgiven your enemies?
Your father and all them?*
All his lifetime of hurt.

I must have (grin). *I don't
think about that now.*

—

People can't say goodbye
any more. They say last hellos.

Going fast, over Christmas,
he'd still stumble out
of his room, where his photos
hang over the other furniture,
and play host to his mourners.

The courage of his bluster,
firm big voice of his confusion.

Two last days in the hospital:
his long forearms were still
red mahogany. His hands
gripped steel frame. *I'm dyin.*

On the second day:
You're bustin to talk
but I'm too busy dyin.

—

Grief ended when he died,
the widower like soldiers who
won't live life their mates missed.

Good boy, Cecil! No more Bluey dog.
No more cowtime. No more stories.
We're still using your imagination,
it was stronger than all ours.

Your grave's got littler
somehow, in the three months.
More pointy as the clay's shrivelled,
like a stuck zip in a coat.

Your cricket boots are in
the State museum! Odd letters

still come. Two more's died since you:
Annie, and Stewart. Old Stewart.

On your day there was a good crowd,
family, and people from away.
But of course a lot had gone
to their own funerals first.

Snobs mind us off religion
nowadays, if they can.
Fuck thém. I wish you God.

All days were work days on the farm:
respite and dreaming were in them,
so holidays, I reasoned in childhood,
must be hollow-days. Which people filled
with hotels, cars, wincing parade sand.
Now my plane is keening in to land
from Hollywood, supreme human judging-ring.

I only looked. Poets are nothing
in that profit vortex. Entertainment
and all the decorations of satiety
were craft, but poetry was a gent
always, regaled with gifts, not money.
Ancient shame, to pay for love or the sacred.
Deny the sacred, and we are owed pay.

Wage justice for poets, a living
like that of all who live off our words:
surreal notions from the lecture I'm giving
uphill from the concrete Liver birds—
then, feasted by kind hosts, I'm away
under Springtime's wind-hoed Mersey
to make holiday amid the ballpoint spires

for new friends and hearers, be well dined
in an ormolu hall, with more good talk in London
till I die of reaction. Not theirs: mine.
Rising, I unzip more high-speed shires,
tour a mansion lovely as an unenraged mind,
nod with narrowboat windows and dipped tyres,
and surface with my family near the Wye, at Hay.

MY ANCESTRESS AND THE SECRET BALLOT

1848 and 1851

Isabella Scott, born eighteen-oh-two,
grows gaunt in a cottage on Cheviot side,
the first and last house in Scotland, its view
like a vast Scottish flag, worn linen and blue
with no warmth in it. When her man died
it's what she and ten children could afford,
out of the village, high in the wind.

Five years before, in Paterson town,
a corpse stains the dust on voting day.
Rioters kicked him to death for the way
he was known to vote; more were struck down.
The way you voted being known
can get you sacked and driven away.
The widened franchise is a fizzer, folk say.

Isabella Scott, when Scotch wives kept
their surnames, has letters from her cousin
in New South Wales, Overseer of Free Men:
*Send me your grown lads. If they adapt
to here, come out yourself with the children.*
In those sunburnt colonies, in more than one mind,
how to repair the ballot's been divined.

Put about, wee ship, on your Great Circle course,
don't carry Bella's Murray daughter and boys
to the British Crown's stolen Austral land.
In ten years the Secret Ballot will force
its way into law in those colonies.
If the poor can just sit on their non-smoking hand
till they're old, help will come from Labor policies

and parties, sprung worldwide from that lag idea
which opens, by evading duellisms of the soul,
the only non-murderous route to the dole.
Don't sail, don't sail, Great-grannie(cubed) dear:
wait just a century and there'll be welfare
in full, and you won't play the Settler role.
The polling booth will be a closet of prayer.

Uphill in Melbourne on a beautiful day
a woman was walking ahead of her hair.
Like teak oiled soft to fracture and sway
it hung to her heels and seconded her
as a pencilled retinue, an unscrolling title
to ploughland, edged with ripe rows of dress,
a sheathed wing that couldn't fly her at all,
only itself, loosely, and her spirits.
                        A largesse
of life and self, brushed all calm and out,
its abstracted attempts on her mouth weren't seen,
nor its showering, its tenting. Just the detail
that swam in its flow-lines, glossing about—
as she paced on, comet-like, face to the sun.

My sleep, that had gone astray
flying home, turned up at last,
developing in the brain's red room
like film of crowding and woollies,
but builders were tapping the house
and I couldn't lie down, not
while they worked. I still can't
do privilege. So I fed the fowls

and pottered round the dead-tree dam
which lay stilled under water fern,
matte as the rough side of masonite
with trails of swimming birds
through it like fading tyre-tracks
and gaps re-coalescing. The cud
of azolla, scooped up, was tiny green
rockery plants, brown only in total.

Wind impulses quivering the water
were damped under that blanket level
which would floor it till next flood.
It made me think of other
dry water. Dry bath water
magicked out of lustrous fine gravel
in the Roman military museum
at Caerleon, in Old South Wales.

The mealiness and illusory slick
of minute stones there evoke steam,
soldier-scrapings and olive oil

worked to motionless ripples, as they fill
the excavated real masonry pools.
Sunproofed water, safety water—yawn.
Imprisoning the actual in commentary:
will that get us sex after death?

Our one-eyed fowl lay on his side
to peck at grain in two dimensions
and, still nailing the house's scansions
and line lengths, the only people
who abash me—*Not a working model,
our bloke! No*—kept me from bed,
atoning for poetry's slight sacredness
and the deep shame of achievement.

An idea whistles with your lips,

laughs with your breath.
An idea hungers for your body.

An alert, hot to dissemble and share,
it snatches up cases of its style
from everywhere, to start a face.

An idea is a mouth that sells
as it sucks. It lusts to have
loomed perpetual in the night colours:
an idea is always a social climb.

Whether still braving snorts,
ordering its shootings, or at rest
among its own charts of world rule,
a maturing idea will suddenly want

to get smaller than its bearers.

It longs to be a poem:
earthed, accurate immortal trance,
buck as stirrups were,
blare as the panther.

Only art can contain an idea.

Shake the bed, the blackened child whimpers,
O shake the bed! through beak lips that never
will come unwry. And wearily the iron-
framed mattress, with nodding crockery bulbs,
jinks on its way.
              Her brothers and sister take
shifts with the terrible glued-together baby
when their unsleeping absolute mother
reels out to snatch an hour, back to stop
the rocking and wring pale blue soap-water
over nude bladders and blood-webbed chars.

Even their cranky evasive father
is awed to stand watches rocking the bed.
Lids frogged shut, *O please shake the bed,*
her contour whorls and braille tattoos
from where, in her nightdress, she flared
out of hearth-drowse to a marrow shriek
pedalling full tilt firesleeves in mid-air,
              are grainier with repair
than when the doctor, crying *Dear God, woman!*
No one can save that child. Let her go!
spared her the treatments of the day.

Shake the bed. Like: count phone poles, rhyme,
classify realities, bang the head, any
iteration that will bring, in the brain's forks,
the melting molecules of relief,
and bring them again.
            O rock the bed!

Nibble water with bared teeth, make lymph
like arrowroot gruel, as your mother grips you
for weeks in the untrained perfect language,
till the doctor relents. Salves and wraps you
in dressings that will be the fire again,
ripping anguish off agony,
                        and will confirm
the ploughland ridges in your woman's skin
for the sixty more years your family weaves you
on devotion's loom, rick-racking the bed
as you yourself, six years old, instruct them.

We came from the Ice Age,
we work for the trances.
The hunter, the Mother,
seers' inside-out glances

come from the Ice Age,
all things in two sexes,
the priest man, the beast man,
I flatten to run
I rise to be human.

We came from the Ice Age
with the walk of the Mothers
with the walk of the powers
we walked where sea now is

we made the dry land
we told it in our trances
we burnt it with our sexes
but the tongue it is sand
see it, all dry taste buds
lapping each foot that crosses
every word is more sand.

Dup dup hey duhn duhn
the rhythm of the Mothers.
We come from the Ice Ages
with the tribes and the trances
the drum's a tapped drone
dup dup hey duhn duhn.

We come from the Ice Age,
poem makers, homemakers,
how you know we are sacred:
it's unlucky to pay us.

Kings are later, farmers later.
After the Ice Age, they
made landscape, made neuter,
they made prose and pay.

Things are bodied by the trances,
we must be paid slant,
loved, analysed and scorned,
the priest's loved in scorn,
how you know he is sacred.

We're gifted and pensioned.
Some paid ones were us:
when they got their wages
ice formed in their mouths
chink chink, the Ice Age.

A prose world is the Ice Age
it is all the one sex
and theory, that floats land
we came over that floe land

we came from the Ice Age
we left it by the trances
worlds warm from the trances

duhn duhn hey dup dup
it goes on, we don't stop
we walk on from the Ice Age.

I must have heard of the Devil
in our splintery church
but the earliest I remember him
is when, as a bullocky's child
in a clan of operatic swearers,
I first essayed the black poetry.

My mouth-farting profanities
horrified Barney McCann,
the Krambach carpenter staying
with us to rebuild our bails:
Lord, I won't sleep on that verandah
where you sleep! Not tonight.
After what you just said
the old Devil's sure to come for you.
O he's bad, with his claws and tail.
My parents smiled uneasily.

Bats flitted, the moon shone in.
Will the old Devil get me?
I quavered, four years old, through the wall,
Will he get me? The agile long-boned man
of pure horror, clinging to the outside
weatherboards like the spur-shouldered
hoatzin bird in my mother's
encyclopedia books. *Not if you*
knock off swearing. Go to sleep, Leslie.

But the carpenter was soldering iron
gutterings, dipping flux with a feather

from a yellow bottle. *Spirits of salts:*
it'll eat through everything. Only
this bottle can hold it. A drop
on your head would sizzle right down
through you, burn on into the ground—
fearful stuff. Then he flicked the feather

at me, and leaned away with a grin
from my wept hysteric shower of oaths.
That's it! I won't sleep in your house now.
He'll take everybody tonight.
I was cured. It became a funny yarn.

But over the next years
I sneaked back, in daylight first,
to the insulted people's language
that made me feel so thrillingly
alone and empty of heart
that the church's doctrines and
the snootiest dismissals of them
would both need to be true
at once, to come near it.
It fitted the future easily.

translated from the German of Heinrich Heine, 1797–1856

In my breast I've seen expire
every worldly vain desire,
even, among things dead in there,
hatred of evil, likewise any care
for my or others' hour of need—
only Death lives in me indeed.
      The curtain falls, the play is done,
and my dear German public as one
saunters yawning in homeward throngs.
The good folk, enjoying laughs and songs
aren't such fools, I have to allow,
supping and boozing and making a row—
It's true, that speech of the noble hero's
long ago in the book Homeros:
the lot of the meanest live Philistine
in Stuttgart-on-Neckar is happier than mine,
I, son of Peleus, dead champ whose shade is
prince of shadows in gloomy Hades.

Against the darker trees or an open car shed
is where we first see rain, on a cumulous day,
a subtle slant locating the light in air
in front of a forties still of tubs and bike-frames.

Next sign, the dust that was white pepper bared
starts pitting and re-knotting into peppercorns.
It stops being a raceway of rocket smoke behind cars,
it sidles off foliage, darkens to a lustre. The roof
of the bush barely leaks yet, but paper slows right down.

Hurrying parcels pearl but don't now split
crossing the carparks. People clap things in odd salute
to the side of their heads, yell wit, dance on their doubles.
The sunny parallels, when opposite the light, have a flung look
like falling seed. They mass, and develop a shore sound:
fixtures get cancelled, the muckiest shovels rack up.

The highway whizzes, and lorries put spin on vapour:
soon puddles hit at speed will arch over you like a slammed
        sea.
I love it all, I agree with it. At nightfall, the cause
of the whole thing revolves, in white and tints, on TV
like the Crab nebula: it brandishes palm trees like mops,
its borders swell over the continent, they compress the other
nations of the weather. Fruit bumps lawn, and every country
        dam

brews under bubbles, milky temperas sombering to oils.
Grass rains upward; the crepe-myrtle tree heels, sopping
        crimson,

needing to be shaken like the kilt of a large man.
Hills run, air and paddocks are swollen. Eaves dribble like
        jaws
and coolness is a silent film, starring green and mirrors.

Tiny firetail finches, quiet in our climber rose, agree to it
like early humans. Cattle agree harder, hunched out in the
        clouds.
From here, the ocean may pump up and up and explode
around the lighthouses in gigantic cloak sleeves, the whole
        book
of foam slide and fritter, disclosing a pen shaft. Paratroops

of salt water may land in dock streets, skinless balloons
be flat out to queue down every drain, and the wind race
thousands of flags. Or we may be just chirpings, damped
under calm high cornfields of pour, with butter clearings

that spread and resume glare, hiding the warm rain
back inside our clothes, as mauve trees scab to cream
and grey trees strip bright salmon, with loden patches.

The Six Million are worth full grief:
it isn't enough to be stunned—
but showing up your elders' multiculture
so easily is what got you shunned,

that, and pity for the greater working class
which their dream made work in the ground,
eighty million in a darkening red flag
outspread under ice, under grass.

No. Not from me. Never.
Not a step in your march,
not a vowel in your unison,
bray that shifts to bay.

Banners sailing a street river,
power in advance of a vote,
go choke on these quatrain tablets.
I grant you no claim ever,

not if you pushed the Christ Child
as president of Rock Candy Mountain
or yowled for the found Elixir
would your caste expectations snare me.

Superhuman with accusation,
you would conscript me to a world
of people spat on, people hiding
ahead of oncoming poetry.

Whatever class is your screen
I'm from several lower.
To your rigged fashions, I'm pariah.
Nothing a mob does is clean,

not at first, not when slowed to a media,
not when police. The first demos I saw,
before placards, were against me,
alone, for two years, with chants,

every day, with half-conciliatory
needling in between, and aloof
moral cowardice holding skirts away.
I learned your world order then.

Two women were characters, continually
rewriting themselves, in turn, with their hands
mostly, but with face and torso too
and very fast, fluttering like the gestures
above a busy street in Shanghai.

Man was a mug, really,
to give them his right age:
I could have gone on
being the lighthouse keeper
for another ten years. Fishing,
lighting her, keeping her clean,
end-for-ending the tablecloth.

A small whale beached below
once. I cut it up for the dogs.
It was good out on the bo'sun's
chair, slathering on paint
with my safety ladder going up,
thinking about cows, and seals,
sand dollars and my wives and stuff.

Queerest thing about the job,
the light that jabs away out
at night, and rides the horizons
comes out of just a bulb
inside this turntable rack
of like thick glass saucers.

When I'd switch her off
of a summer morning
and polish those ridgy lenses
I had to draw the curtains
round the windows facing inland
or else the sun could spike in
through them, the lenses, and make
rays, and set all the bush alight.

for Sir John Guise

In many a powerless mind
lurks this chart, wider than the world,
maybe vast enough to wrap Earth in,
which diagrams with merciless truth
the parentage of everyone, identified
and linked with their real blood kin
across all of time and space.

Strips and fragments of this
have always been waved, in ribaldry
or secret, at Identity overdone,
that is, underdone with intent—
wives have hung them out with the smalls,
Hitler sent Panzers to train
all over his, for Gentility.

Certain knowledge or the insurrection
of guesswork, month-counter's revenge, the
mugging of high sentence by and with
its impossible relations—plenty
if they could get the true chart
wouldn't care that to display it entire
might be ridiculous and terrible:

Howls of revised posh, unspoken people,
cousinship with kulak-shooters, death-rays
of Whititude and Negritude, burning wills,
anguish of men out of whose children
other men peer innocently,
shock historical non-paternities

and the stratosphere-tightening
gasp at incest seen in full.

Glorious to see a hero car-bomber
shattered by wrong ancestry, a Klan klutz
awed by strata of peoples, all his,
or an adoptee hunched, devouring names,
but the chart would need to hang
in Space, to be safe from us,
like the relativised stars, which were
once also made by love.

A million years' unreachable blamed dead
might stun revenge, sheer wealth of tangents
heal affinity and victimhood:
an Indigenous poet might regain her
Hispano-Scots Kanak dimensions, as her
scorners darkly complexified.
She's your aunt a thousand generations
before your sealblubber aunts, Son of Heaven.

A species-deep net of anecdote
with every life its pardon.
In that weak Force I'm one eighth
of a musketeer, being slightly a Dumas
on my Aboriginal side. The chart is always
odder than reincarnation's princess tales
with truncations and tears. It's the galaxy
we are making, the kinship sum:
I'm game to see it. I want it to come.

The houses those suburbs could afford
were roofed with old savings books, and some
seeped gravy at stitches in their walls;

some were clipped as close as fury,
some grimed and corner-bashed by love
and the real estate, as it got more vacant,

grew blady grass and blowfly grass, so called
for the exquisite lanterns of its seed,
and the land sagged subtly to a low point,

it all inclined way out there to a pit
with burnt-looking cheap marble edges
and things and figures flew up from it

like the stones in the crusher Piers had
for making dusts of them for glazes:
flint, pyroclase, slickensides, quartz, schist,

snapping, refusing, and spitting high
till the steel teeth got gritty corners on them
and could grip them craw-chokingly to grind.

It's their chance, a man with beerglass-cut arms
told me. Those hoppers got to keep filled. A girl,
edging in, bounced out cropped and wrong-coloured

like a chemist's photo, crying. Who could blame her
among in-depth grabs and Bali flights and phones?
She was true, and got what truth gets.

The children pouring down,
supervised, into the ravine
and talking animatedly all over
each other like faces in a payout
of small change, now come in
under a vast shadowy marquee
of native fig and tree of heaven.
In their indigo and white
they flow on down, glimpsed
between the patisserie trunks
of green coral trees, and as
they go on towards the ocean
they are still tangling and grabbing
at an elusive bright string
that many want to pick off others
and off themselves. It is
of course childhood, which they
scorn as a disabling naïveté
even under the enchanted rotation
of gun-sleeved sky-propellor trees.

Where I lived once, a roller coaster's range
of timber hills peaked just by our backyard cliff
and cars undulated scream-driven round its seismograph
and climbed up to us with an indrawn gasp of girls.

Smiles and yelling could be exchanged as they crested
then they'd pitch over, straining back in a shriek
that volleyed as the cars were snatched from sight
in the abyss, and were soon back. Weekdays they rested,

and I rested all days. There was a spider in my head
I'd long stay unaware of. If you're raped you mostly know
but I'd been cursed, and refused to notice or believe it.
Aloof in a Push squat, I thought I was moral, or dead.

Misrule was strict there, and the Pill of the day only ever
went into one mouth, not mine, and foamed a Santa-beard.
I was resented for chastity, and slept on an overcoat.
Once Carol from upstairs came to me in bra and kindness

and the spider secreted by girls' derision-rites to spare
women from me had to numb me to a crazed politeness.
Squeals rode the edge of the thrill building. Cartoonist
    Mercier
drew springs under Sydney. Push lovers were untrue on
    principle.

It's all architecture over there now. A new roller coaster
flies its ups and downs in wealth's face like an affront.
I've written a new body that only needs a reader's touch.
If love is cursed in us, then when God exists, we don't.

The Push: An Australian bohemia existing from the 1940s to the 1970s. Nominally libertarian, it in fact enforced a fairly pedantic inversion of ordinary norms and practices. Its most famous alumna is Germaine Greer.

Streaming, a hippo surfaces
like the head of someone
lifting, with still-entranced eyes,
from a lake of stanzas.